Skills Map

Why research?

Understand the need to use other sources of information to strengthen your essays.

The research process

Familiarise yourself with the range of sources of information and consider their strengths and weaknesses.

Writing a bibliography

Understand the use and importance of a bibliography and learn the basics of writing one in the APA system.

Referring to other sources in your essay

Understand the uses of quotations and citations and familiarise yourself with the APA system of referencing.

Plagiarism

Understand what plagiarism is and how to recognise it in a piece of writing so that you can use other sources in your writing in an acceptable way.

Using supporting arguments

Identify relevant information in your research notes and understand how to use it in your essay to support arguments in an acceptable way.

Destination: Research and Referencing

1 Why research?

At the end of this unit you will:
- understand the need to refer to other sources;
- be aware of different conventions and attitudes to research in different cultures.

Task 1 Why research?

1.1 Imagine you are going to write an essay on homelessness. In groups of 3–5, spend 10 minutes discussing homelessness.

a) What is homelessness?

b) How big a problem do you think it is?

c) What causes homelessness?   *poverty, unemployment, housing shortage, violence mental drug*

d) What impact does it have on individuals and society?   *phys & mental health, sense of identity, social integration, academic perf.*

e) What can be done to address the problem?   *tackle root causes*

1.2 Now discuss the following questions with your whole class.

a) How much did you know about homelessness before your discussion?

b) What have you learnt from the discussion?

c) What extra information or ideas would you need to know to write an essay on homelessness?

d) What sources of information could help you write this essay?

Task 2 Supporting evidence and arguments

2.1 Read the essay on the next page and underline the answers to these questions.

a) How big is the problem of homelessness?

b) What are its main causes?

c) What are its effects?

d) Can homelessness be alleviated?

What are the causes and impacts of homelessness?
by Andrew Student

One of the world's most pressing problems is that of homelessness. In recent years, there has been a dramatic rise in the number of people who have found themselves living on the streets.

Andrew Student

Homelessness can be defined as the condition of people who lack regular access to adequate housing. This problem can affect a wide range of people, including children, the elderly and, in some cases, whole families.

People become homeless for many reasons, including poverty, a lack of employment, a shortage of affordable housing, domestic violence, mental illness and drug addiction.

Homelessness has a profound effect on those who experience it. It is likely to have a negative impact on physical and mental health, sense of identity and social integration. In the case of homeless children, academic performance may be impaired as well.

Homelessness is clearly becoming an urgent problem, given the increasing number of people who are affected and the severity of its impact on individuals and society. To address the problem, its root causes need to be targeted, rather than just its symptoms. Otherwise, the problem of homelessness will simply be perpetuated.

2.2 **In your groups, discuss the following questions and write notes.**

a) What new information have you learnt about homelessness?

b) Has the writer shown a good knowledge of the topic?

c) Do you agree with the definition of homelessness?

d) How convincing is the argument in this essay?

2.3 **Work individually. Underline the parts of the essay where you could add supporting points and evidence to strengthen the essay. Then compare with a partner.**

Task 3 Academic cultures

3.1 **The following comments were made by four international students at British universities. Read about their experiences and discuss the questions below with your partner.**

a) Have you had similar experiences?

b) What are the main differences between university writing in the UK and in these students' countries?

c) How do the international students feel about these differences?

d) What advice would you give them?

Kris:

In my country, we don't do much writing at undergraduate level. We go to lectures, take notes and learn the information. At the end of the year we have an exam, but it's spoken. In England, you have to do so many essays. At first I found it strange, but now I like it as the essays make me think about the topics we are studying and I can use the essays to help me revise for exams.

Bo:

I am a science student, and the way we write our reports is so different to how people do it here in the UK. One thing is the length. In the UK, writers add a lot of stuff which is totally irrelevant and boring. The beginnings and the ends of the reports are full of quotations from other people's research. In my country, we talk about the problem, the methodology and the solution. There is no point talking about other people's work. It's in the library and a good student knows it already. It is boring to mention it again.

Edward:

I didn't write a bibliography (a list of sources) until I was writing a long essay in my final year. Before that, my tutors didn't require one. After I had finished writing the essay, I just put all the books I had used in a big pile on my desk and wrote out their details in a list. My only problem when I'm writing in English is that I have to keep stopping to add a reference and make sure the book is in my bibliography too. Sometimes, it makes me forget my ideas.

Phan:

In my country, we are taught not to steal other people's ideas or writing. So when we do university writing, we write a list of all the books we have used in a bibliography. We don't give a reference in the text of our essay. It's enough to mention the books in our bibliographies. Also, if the idea is well known or if it comes from a lecture, we don't mention it in a bibliography because the tutors and students know where the idea is from. At first, I kept forgetting this type of thing in my bibliographies, but now I am beginning to change.

In this unit you have learnt about the importance of researching sources to support your arguments. This will clearly lead to extra work, particularly as you need to make reference to sources. It is important that you work out your attitude to this right from the beginning.

First of all, think about how important it is to refer to other sources in the academic culture of your country. If what you are used to is very different, you will need to find good reasons to change. The most basic reason is that you have to accept the change, rather than fight it, to ensure that you get a good diploma or degree at the end of your studies.

But a more positive way of looking at this issue is that higher educational study is an opportunity to broaden your learning. The more you have to put into your studies, the more you will get out of them. Once you get used to research and referencing, you will probably find that the benefits outweigh the drawbacks.

Reflect carefully on these issues and decide where you stand and where you feel your best interests lie.

Student notes for Unit 1

2 The research process

At the end of this unit you will:
- be aware of a range of sources of information;
- be able to identify the strengths and weaknesses of different sources;
- be able to note down bibliographical details for books and websites.

Task 1 Research options

1.1 Work in groups of 3–5. Look at the list of sources of information below and discuss which ones you have already used. Add to the list any other sources of information that you are familiar with.

a) books

b) websites

c) journals

d) *articles*

e) *newspapers*

f) *theses*

g) *TV progs*

1.2 In your group, discuss the strengths and weaknesses of the different sources of information in your list above. Refer to your own experience of using these various sources. Make notes in the table on the following page.

You should consider:

a) authority

b) ease of access

c) reliability

d) amount of information

e) relevance

f) time

What else might you consider?

Source	Strengths	Weaknesses
books		
websites		
journals		

Task 2 Preparing research questions

Now you are going to write a list of sources (a bibliography) that could be used to strengthen Andrew Student's essay on homelessness.

2.1 **Look back at your notes to Task 2.2 in Unit 1. Identify what information would be useful.**

For example:

Definitions of homelessness, size of the problem

2.2 **Turn these notes into three research questions and write them below. Leave space after each question to add notes and sources later on.**

For example:

How has homelessness been defined by other writers? What information indicates the size of the problem?

Research question 1:
Notes:
Reference sources:

Research question 2:
Notes:
Reference sources:

Research question 3:
Notes:
Reference sources:

Task 3 Information for a bibliography

You are going to find some sources to answer your research questions and write a bibliography. This is a complete list of sources which have been used to prepare an essay, and it usually appears at the end of an essay. It is important to keep a note of the bibliographical information. Without this information, you cannot use the source in your essay.

3.1 To find the necessary bibliographical information for a book, look on the title page and the printing history page (usually on the first few pages of a book). Below are examples of these.

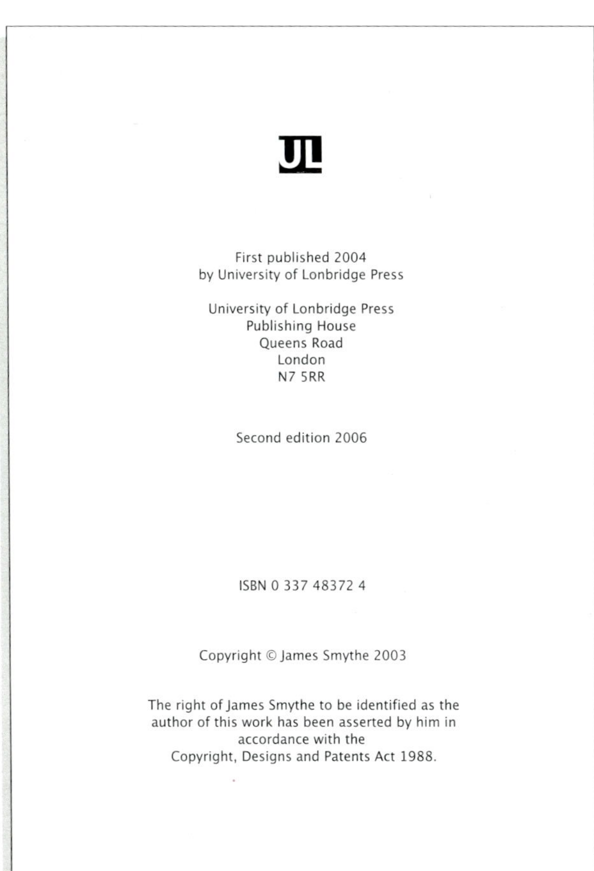

Find the following bibliographical information and then compare your answers with a partner.

a) Author's full name

b) Date of publication

c) Title

d) Edition

e) Place of publication

f) Publisher

3.2   A bibliography also includes any websites you used to research your essay.

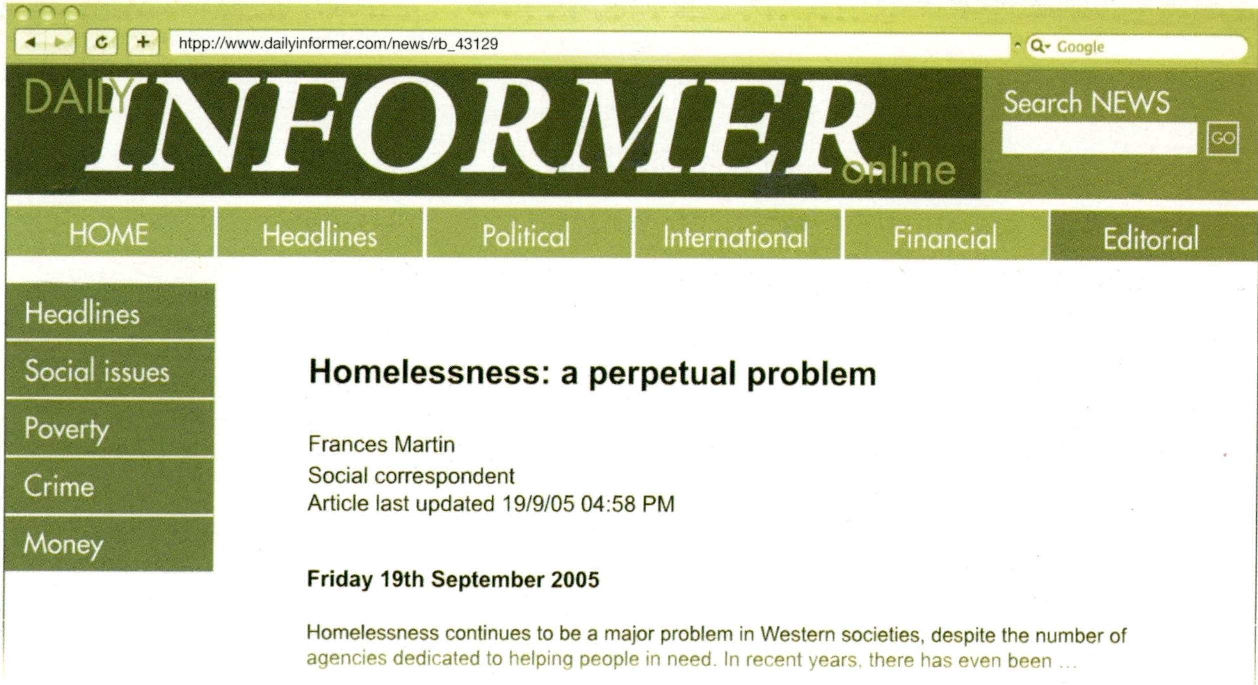

Find the following bibliographical information and then compare your answers with a partner.

a)   Author's full name

b)   Date the information was last updated

c)   Title

d)   Web address: http://

3.3   **You might need to look carefully to find when a website was last updated. Type the following into a search engine and see how each one is organised: homeless+last updated.**

3.4   **Ask your tutor or a librarian for help with the bibliographical details you need to have for other types of information source. Alternatively, the Internet is a good source of information on writing bibliographies.**

Task 4 Researching

4.1   Use a library to find two books and two websites which help answer the research questions you wrote in Task 2.2. During this task, think about the reliability and authority of your sources.

Look back at the research questions you wrote in 2.2 and add brief notes after each one. Keep a record of the bibliographical details of your source on the same page as your notes.

4.2   From your notes, write down the bibliographical details for your sources in the table on the next page.

Tips

a)   Most libraries now make use of electronic search engines. If you are not familiar with them, ask a librarian for help.

b)   You can use a search engine such as Google or Yahoo to find relevant sites.

http://google.co.uk
http://yahoo.co.uk

c)   You can also use web directories.

http://www.lycos.co.uk/dir/
http://dir.yahoo.com/

d)   Subject gateways are also a good source of information. The sources are divided up according to academic subjects.

http://www.intute.ac.uk/

e)   You can also make use of the links provided by Society Guardian at:

http://society.guardian.co.uk/homelessness/page/0,8149,527295,00.html

Or by the UK government at:

http://www.odpm.gov.uk/stellent/groups/opdmhomelessness/documents/sectionhomepage/
odpm homelessness page.hcsp
http://www.communities.gov.uk/index.asp?id=1149659

Books

Author's family name and initial	Date of publication	Title	Edition	Place of publication	Publisher

Websites

Author's family name and initial	When last updated	Title	Date you accessed the site	Web address
				http://
				http://

Reflect

There are a variety of reasons for referring to sources in your writing. For example, you might use them when:

- giving factual information;
- providing examples;
- referring to relevant theories;
- presenting an argument or counterargument;
- supporting your own argument or counterargument.

Think about the research you carried out into homelessness. Which types of information did you tend to look for? Did you look for any other information types?

Now consider your future studies. Do you think you will tend to use the same information types, or more of a variety?

Student notes for Unit 2

Writing a bibliography

At the end of this unit you will:
- understand the purpose of a bibliography;
- be able to produce a bibliography using the APA System.

Task 1 Why include a bibliography?

1.1 In groups of 3–5, spend 10 minutes discussing bibliographies.

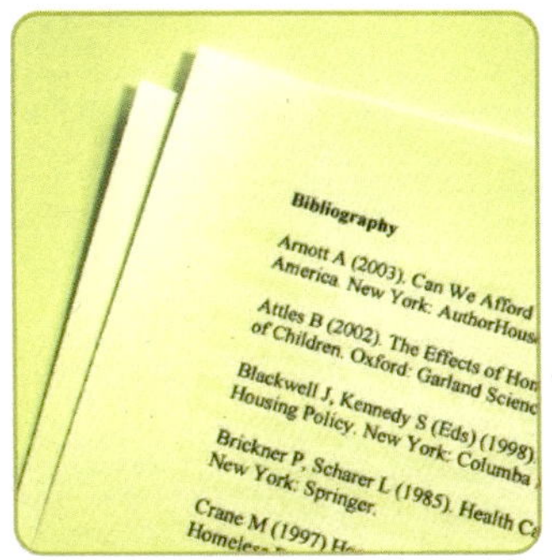

a) How much experience have you had of writing bibliographies in the past?

b) Why is a bibliography useful for the reader?

c) Why is writing a bibliography useful for you, the writer?

1.2 Now think about when you found sources to strengthen Andrew Student's essay on homelessness. Discuss the following questions with your class.

a) How did you use the bibliographies you found in the sources for the homelessness essay?

b) Why is it important for a bibliography to be complete and accurate?

Task 2 Bibliographies and the APA System

2.1 There are many different systems of citation, and they often differ from one academic field to another. In this exercise you will practise one of the most widely used ones – the APA System. The example below shows this system.

Bibliography

Morris, J. & Winn, M. (1990). *Housing and social inequality.* London: Longman.

O'Dwyer, C. (1994). *Homelessness: what's the problem?* 2nd ed. London: Shelter.

Ratcliffe, P. (1997a). *Housing in Bradford, Bradford Housing Forum.* Oxford: Oxford University Press.

Ratcliffe, P. (1997b). *Race, ethnicity and housing differentials in Britain.* London: Blackwell.

Scottish Homes. (1997). *Home owners in Scotland.* Edinburgh: University of Edinburgh.

Use the bibliography to answer the following questions:

a) What is the name of the book which was written by Caroline O'Dwyer?

b) When was *Housing and social inequality* published?

c) Who published *Race, ethnicity and housing differentials in Britain*?

d) What does *2nd ed.* mean in the entry for *Homelessness: what's the problem*?

e) Where was *Home owners in Scotland* published?

f) What did Jenny Morris and Martin Winn write?

g) What do the letters *a* and *b* mean in the entries for the books written by Peter Ratcliffe?

h) If a book has two authors, how is the entry written?

i) If the book is written by a corporate author (e.g., an organisation, a government department), what information comes first in the entry?

j) In which order should entries be placed?

2.2 **Look at the examples in the bibliography on page 15. What are the rules for writing a bibliographical entry for a book? Consider the order of information and punctuation.**

2.3 **Take the book sources you found in Unit 2, Task 4.2. Using the rules you have discovered, write bibliographical entries for your sources.**

Task 3 Bibliographies and electronic sources

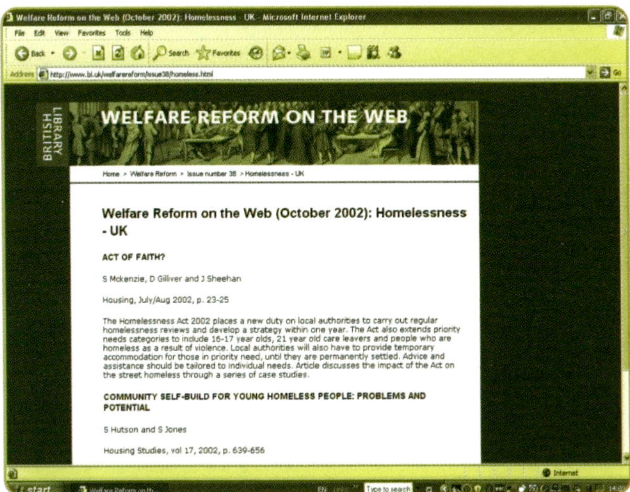

There is an increasing amount of information available on the Internet. This kind of information can be a valuable source, but it is important to use it correctly.

Before you use an electronic source in your essay, you need to decide if it is reliable. The publishing of a book is a much more careful process than the publishing of a website. You should use reliable sites, for example the official sites of universities or well-known companies.

As the three examples below show, the bibliographical rules for electronic sources differ slightly from books. It is important to give the address of the page, not just the address of the website. You can copy this from the browser window.

Grassian, E. (2000). *Thinking critically about World Wide Web resources.*
Retrieved October 24, 2006, from http://www.library.ucla.edu/libraries/college/help/critical/index.htm

Department for communities and local government (n.d.). *Overview of homelessness data.*
Retrieved 24 October, 2006, from http://www.communities.gov.uk/index.asp?id=1156292

Society Guardian. (2005). *The most useful websites on homelessness.*
Retrieved 24 October, 2006, from
http://society.guardian.co.uk/homelessness/page/0,8149,527295,00.html

3.1   Use the bibliography above to answer the following questions.

a) When was *Thinking critically about World Wide Web resources* written?

b) When did the writer of the bibliography visit the site *Thinking critically about World Wide Web resources*?

c) Why does *Overview of homelessness data* not have a family name and initial as an author?

d) When was the site *The most useful websites on homelessness* last updated?

e) What information suggests that *Thinking critically about World Wide Web resources* is a reliable source?

f) What does (n.d.) mean in the *Overview of homelessness data* entry?

3.2   Look at the examples of Internet source entries in the bibliography on page 17. What are the rules for writing a bibliographical entry for a website page?

3.3   Take the Internet sources you found in Unit 2, Task 4.2, and put them into the format shown above.

3.4   Work in groups of 3–5. Discuss the following questions and write notes.

a) Why do you include the date you accessed a website in a bibliography?

b) How reliable are the websites you chose to use for the homelessness essay?

Reflect

Think of how much use you made of bibliographies before starting your higher education studies. Compare that with the use you are beginning to make of them now.

Reflect on how useful you have found bibliographies since beginning your studies. Have you used them for follow-up research? Have you checked the dates of sources cited? Have you checked to see what else the authors have written?

Try to imagine your future studies. Do you think there will be a significant increase in your use of bibliographies?

Student notes for Unit 3

Unit 4 — Referring to other sources in your essay

At the end of this unit you will:
- understand how to decide between citing and quoting;
- be able to acknowledge your sources in the body of your essay.

Citing and quoting are two methods of referring to other sources in your essays.

Task 1 Citing

According to Shaks Ghosh (2006), people are isolated and de-skilled by homelessness.

Shaks Ghosh
Tuesday July 18, 2006
The Guardian

Homelessness de-skills and isolates people. The obvious response is to give homeless people homes …

Citing is reporting ideas or information from another source using your own words. This differs from copying verbatim (exactly word for word) and without acknowledgement, for two reasons. First, you can select and summarise important points from the source. Secondly, you make it clear from whom and where you got your ideas.

To avoid copying another writer's words directly into your essay by mistake, good note-taking technique is important. Using keywords, symbols and paraphrasing at the note-taking stage all make it less likely to copy by mistake. It is also vital to write down the bibliographical details of the source accurately.

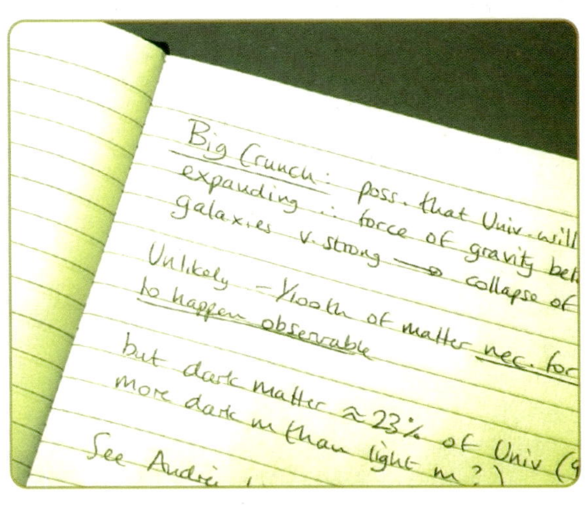

Look at this example.

Bibliographical entry for the source:

Grassian, E. (2000). *Thinking critically about World Wide Web resources.*
Retrieved October 24, 2006, from http://www.library.ucla.edu/libraries/college/help/critical/index.htm

Exact sentence from the source:

'The World Wide Web has a lot to offer, but not all sources are equally valuable or reliable.'

Citing the source in an essay

According to Grassian (2000), Internet sources vary in accuracy and usefulness.

Or

In her evaluation of websites, Grassian (2000) argues that Internet sources vary in accuracy and usefulness.

1.1 **Discuss these questions with your partner.**

a) How original is Grassian's idea?

b) Why has the essay writer used Grassian's idea in the essay?

c) How has the essay writer shown whose idea is given?

d) Why doesn't the essay writer include Grassian's initial (E.)?

e) How has the essay writer shown the reader where to find Grassian's idea?

f) What changes did the essay writer make in order to avoid copying Grassian's text word for word?

1.2 **In groups of 3–5, discuss the following questions.**

a) Why is the APA style widely used?

b) Have you used a similar system before?

c) Why is it better to add the author and date information to your essay at the same time as you write your essay, rather than after you have finished writing it?

Task 2 Quoting

Quoting is another method of reporting the ideas from another source. Unlike citing, you may use the exact words of the source's writer. Similar to citing, however, you make sure your reader understands who the words belong to and in which source they appear.

As a rule, quotations are used less often than citations. One reason for quoting is when you feel the author expresses an idea or opinion in such a way that it is particularly succinct, memorable or interesting. For example:

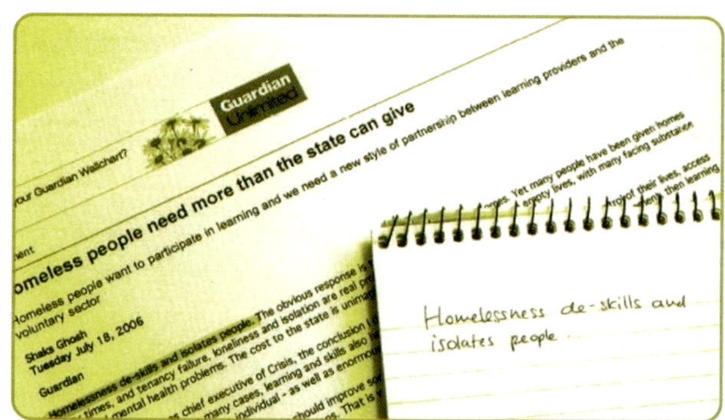

Quoting the source in an essay

A number of studies (Anderson & Thompson, 2005; Fitzpatrick, 2000) have found that young homeless people's definitions of homelessness differ from the definition used by the government, which is discussed above. One interviewee says, 'I think I was homeless, not because I was living in the street, basically because we, me and my sister, were living at a different house every week and basically living out of a bag in that house' (Anderson & Thompson 2005, p. 21).

2.1 **Discuss with your partner.**

   a) Why did the essay writer decide to quote, rather than paraphrase, Anderson and Thompson's text?

   b) Which words are from Anderson and Thompson's text?

   c) Which words are the essay writer's words?

   d) How do you know which words are from Anderson and Thompson's text?

   e) Why has the essay writer included 2005 in brackets?

   f) What does p. 21 mean and why has the essay writer included this information?

2.2 **A second reason for quoting is to strengthen your own argument by referring to an authority. Look at the references below. Then discuss the questions with a partner.**

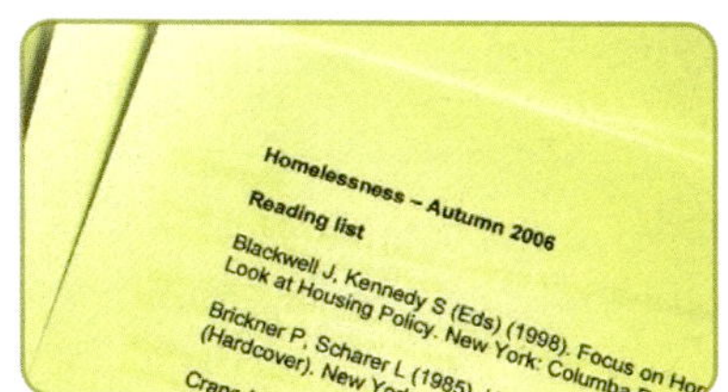

Bibliographical entry for the source
Fitzpatrick, S., Kemp, P., & Klinker, S. (2000). *Single homelessness: An overview of research in Britain*. Bristol: The Policy Press and Joseph Rowntree Foundation*

Quoting the source in an essay
Fitzpatrick et al. (2000, p. 121) define homelessness as a 'lack of right to or access to … secure and minimally adequate housing space'.

*The Joseph Rowntree Foundation is one of the largest social policy research and development charities in the UK.

   a) Why might the authors of *Single homelessness: An overview of research in Britain* be authorities on the subject of homelessness?

   b) What does *et al.* mean and when is it used?

   c) In the middle of the quotation there are three dots (…). What does this punctuation mean?

2.3 **The layout of a long quotation is different to the examples of short quotations above. A long quotation is usually considered to be three or more lines of text. Look at the example below. Then discuss the questions on the next page.**

Adam Sampson, director of Shelter, made the following comment in response to the homelessness statistics issued by the government:

Although the number of people being accepted as homeless has fallen, the fact remains there are still record numbers of people trapped in temporary accommodation, and hundreds of thousands more in overcrowded or unfit housing. (Sampson 2005).

From this, it can be seen that Sampson is aware that the new statistics may be used to give the misleading impression that homelessness is no longer a pressing problem.

a) How are the layout and punctuation of a long quotation different from those of a short quotation?

b) What is the maximum length of a quotation?

c) It is usual for a quotation to be followed by a page number in the in-text reference, but in this example there isn't one. When is it possible not to give a page number?

2.4 **In groups of 3–5, discuss the following questions.**

a) What is the difference between the following uses of the same source?

According to Weller (1949, p. 87), 'East, west, home is best …'

Weller (1949) believes that it doesn't matter where one travels to, in the end most people prefer their homes.

b) Why is citing usually preferable to quoting?

c) What is your tutor's view likely to be if you link together long but accurately acknowledged quotations with a few words of your own in your essay?

d) What is your tutor likely to think if you don't represent a source writer's ideas or opinions accurately in your writing?

e) What may happen if you don't acknowledge that an idea or a quotation belongs to another writer?

Task 3 Citing and quoting practice

3.1 **Work individually. Look at your sources about homelessness. Underline two important points and copy them verbatim (word for word) into the box below. Make notes in the box too. Use keywords and symbols and change the language of the source text as much as possible.**

Using your notes, write two citations. Try to use both book and Internet sources.

Citation:

The words in the source:

Your notes:

Citation 1

<table>
<tr><td>Citation:</td></tr>
<tr><td>The words in the source:</td></tr>
<tr><td>Your notes:</td></tr>
</table>

Citation 2:

<table>
<tr><td>Citation:</td></tr>
<tr><td>The words in the source:</td></tr>
<tr><td>Your notes:</td></tr>
</table>

3.2   **Work with your partner. Discuss the following questions.**

   a)   Do your partner's citations change the meaning of the source?

   b)   Has your partner clearly changed the language of the source?

   c)   Has your partner given an accurate in-text reference?

3.3   **Work individually. Find two examples in your sources that you could quote in an essay on homelessness. Write them in the boxes below as they would appear in your essay. Try to use both book and Internet sources.**

Quotation:

Quotation:

3.4 **Work with your partner. Discuss the following questions.**

a) Why has your partner decided to quote, rather than paraphrase, these parts of the source text?

b) Has your partner acknowledged the source accurately?

Task 4 Referencing practice

4.1 **Working in groups of 3–5, read the passage below and underline the sections which have not been properly referenced. Then compare your work.**

In a recent article on homelessness in London, an expert analysed the reasons behind the growing numbers of homeless people in the city and concluded that drug abuse was the primary cause of homelessness amongst young people. This claim is, however, questioned by another academic on the website www.homeless.co.uk. According to the second author, the first author's statement that drug abuse is common amongst homeless people under the age of 20 is not supported by the statistical evidence provided by the National Statistics Bureau.

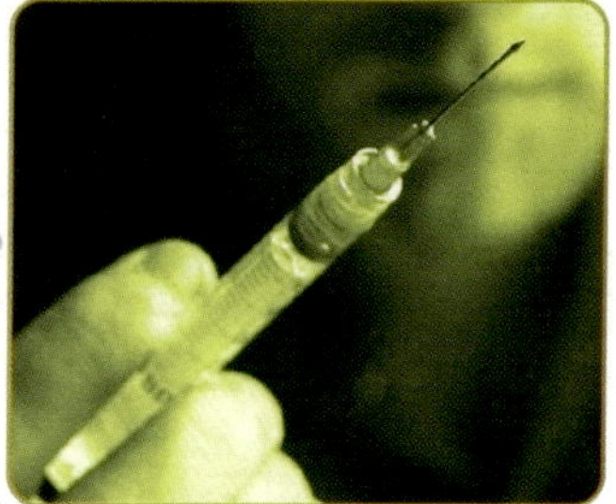

Reflect

When citing from a source, you need to make sure you use your own words. Think about the way you paraphrase from sources at the moment.

Can you think of any steps you could take to improve the way you do this and ensure that you do not steal the source writer's language or ideas by mistake? Think about note-taking, the use of vocabulary, different ways of constructing sentences and any other ideas that might help.

Student notes for Unit 4

Plagiarism

At the end of this unit you will:
- understand what plagiarism is;
- understand how to use sources in your writing;
- be able to recognise plagiarism in a piece of writing.

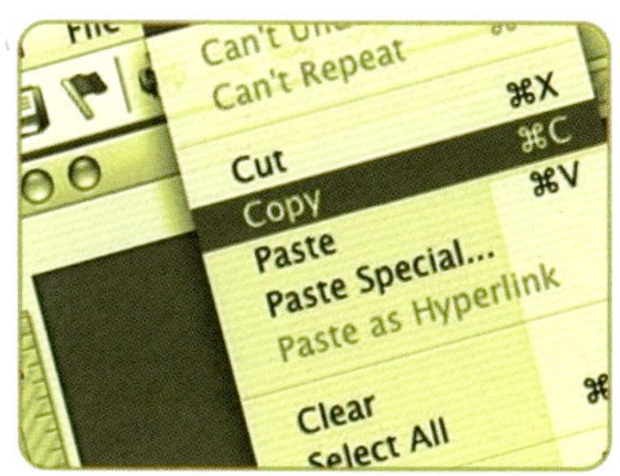

Task 1 What is plagiarism?

1.1 **In groups of 3–5, discuss your answers to the following questions.**

a) Why is it necessary to refer to other sources when writing an essay or report?

b) What do you understand by the term 'plagiarism'?

The origin of the word 'plagiarism' is a Latin word meaning 'a thief'. Plagiarism is a type of academic theft, in which ideas and/or language are stolen from someone else. In its most obvious form, plagiarism involves the word-for-word copying of large sections of another person's material with no indication of the original source. Because of the lack of in-text reference, the plagiarist is claiming the ideas and language as his or her own.

In a less extreme form, the plagiarist copies shorter phrases from a source and links these together with his or her own words. This is also plagiarism if there is no in-text reference to show that the ideas come from another source or if there are no quotation marks around shorter quotations to show that the words belong to someone else. In scientific subjects, plagiarism could also be copying another person's results, calculations or program code, perhaps with minor changes in accuracy, explanation, layout or identifiers.

 **Plagiarism is a form of cheating and is liable to punishment.**

1.2 **Read the text above. In groups of 3–5, discuss your answers to the following questions.**

a) What is the difference between plagiarism and acceptable reference to other sources?

b) Why do tutors take plagiarism so seriously?

c) Has the Internet made plagiarism easier?

d) Is plagiarism a problem just for non-native speaker students?

e) What might the penalty be if you plagiarise a piece of assessed work?

Task 2 Plagiarism and other misuses of sources

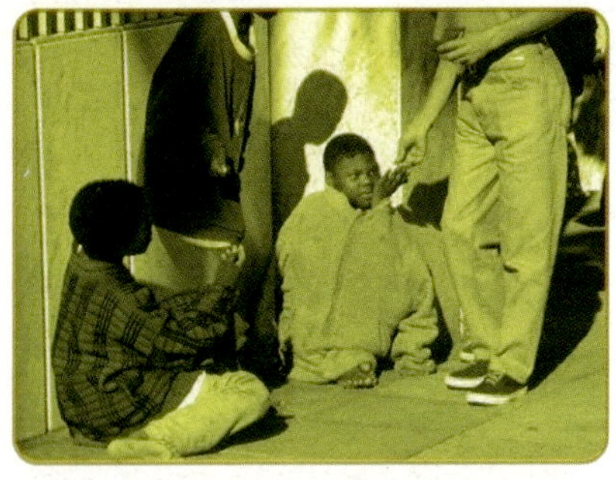

2.1 **Look at how four writers have used a source text in a paragraph in their essays. Discuss your answers to the questions below in your group.**

a) How has each writer used the language of the source?

b) How has each writer used the ideas from the source?

c) Which paragraphs show the writer has understood the ideas in the source?

d) Which of the four paragraphs is not plagiarised?

Source text

Forrester G. (2006) Push factors in youth homelessness. 3rd ed. Reading: Garnet

A paragraph taken from p. 22

Push factors account for a high proportion of youth homelessness, possibly as much as 80% (Centrepoint 2005). Push factors tend to make young people leave home without much pre-planning, leaving them vulnerable. These factors may be interpersonal, for example disputes with family members, family break-ups, and various forms of violence. Push factors may also be related to lack of resources in the shape of poverty or lack of space in the family home. Young people affected by push factors tend to leave home before the age of 16 and consequently often lack the skills and resources to set up their own home. A recent survey found that over 40% of the young homeless interviewees had no formal qualifications and 24% had no source of income (Centrepoint 2005).

Paragraphs

(a) *Push factors account for a high proportion of youth homelessness. Possibly as many as 8 out of 10 young homeless people leave home because of push factors, which include disputes with family members, violence and poverty (Centrepoint 2005). Push factors tend to make young people leave home without much pre-planning, leaving them vulnerable. Young people affected by push factors tend to leave home before the age of 16 and consequently often lack the skills and resources to set up their own home.*

(b) *Push factors in youth homelessness may be divided into two categories: 'interpersonal' factors and factors relating to a shortage of resources (Forrester 2006, p. 22). In the UK, these factors play a significant role in young people becoming homeless. According to a survey carried out by the London-based charity, Centrepoint, approximately 80% of cases of youth homelessness are the result of push factors (Centrepoint 2005 cited in Forrester 2006).*

(c) *Push factors cause a large proportion of homelessness, approximately 80% (Centrepoint 2005). Push factors are inclined to make juveniles leave home without much pre-planning, leaving them weak. These factors might be interpersonal, for instance disputes with relatives, relations break-ups and a mixture of forms of violence. Push factors may also be interconnected to lack of wealth in the nature of lack or not having enough space in the family home. Young people exaggerated by push factors tend to leave home before the age of 16 and so often lack the skills and resources to set up their own abode. A recent survey found that over 40% of the young destitute interviewees had no strict qualifications and 24% had no cause of income (Centrepoint 2005).*

(d) *Forester (2005) states that push factors can be categorised in two groups: interpersonal factors, such as arguments with other members of the family and violence within the home on the one hand and resource-related factors, such as lack of money or sufficient living space on the other. She adds that these push factors often cause young people to leave the family home before they are 16, with the result that these young people are particularly at risk because they may have no recognised qualifications.*

Notes

Your paragraph

Reflect

Think about the various reasons that students plagiarise. Some possible reasons are given below:

- Lack of confidence
- Laziness
- Trying to impress
- Other students do it
- It's not really wrong
- Lecturers encourage it

Which ones do you think are valid? Which are more common? What other reasons can you think of?

When you have come up with a clear list, carry out the following procedure. Imagine that you are a tutor on your course discussing the issue with a group of students. The group of students gives reasons for plagiarising from your list. Find ways of countering their arguments.

Student notes for Unit 5

Unit 6 — Using supporting arguments

At the end of this unit you will:

- be able to select relevant information from your research notes;
- be able to support your arguments;
- be able to acknowledge your sources acceptably.

Task 1 Using supporting statements

This final unit asks you to strengthen Andrew Student's essay (Unit 1, Task 2.1). To do this, you will select relevant information from your research notes and add this support to the argument.

1.1 **Below is the essay on homelessness written by Andrew Student. Andrew has some good ideas, but he has not given enough data, examples and supporting points. To get a good mark, he will have to support his argument with statements and ideas from other sources.**

Using your notes from Unit 1, Task 2.2, put an arrow and a number where the argument needs support.

What are the causes and impacts of homelessness?
by Andrew Student

Andrew Student

One of the world's most pressing problems is that of homelessness. In recent years, there has been a dramatic rise in the number of people who have found themselves living on the streets.

Homelessness can be defined as the condition of people who lack regular access to adequate housing. This problem can affect a wide range of people, including children, the elderly and, in some cases, whole families.

People become homeless for many reasons, including poverty, a lack of employment, a shortage of affordable housing, domestic violence, mental illness and drug addiction.

Homelessness has a profound effect on those who experience it. It is likely to have a negative impact on physical and mental health, sense of identity and social integration. In the case of homeless children, academic performance may be impaired as well.

Homelessness is clearly becoming an urgent problem, given the increasing number of people who are affected and the severity of its impact on individuals and society. To address the problem, its root causes need to be targeted, rather than just its symptoms. Otherwise, the problem of homelessness will simply be perpetuated.

1.2   Look at the notes you made from your sources to answer your research questions (Unit 2, Task 4.1). Choose the most relevant information to support Andrew Student's argument. This will probably include examples, statistical data and more specific points which support his argument.

1.3   Decide which information needs quoting and which needs citing.

1.4   Write each citation and quotation in the appropriate box below the excerpt. Number each one to match the arrows and numbers you have added to the essay. Make sure that all the citations and quotations are correctly referenced.

1.5   Write a bibliography for the sources you have used in APA style.

What are the causes and impacts of homelessness? – by Andrew Student

One of the world's most pressing problems is that of homelessness. In recent years, there has been a dramatic rise in the number of people who have found themselves living on the streets.

Homelessness can be defined as the condition of people who lack regular access to adequate housing. This problem can affect a wide range of people, including children, the elderly and, in some cases, whole families.

People become homeless for many reasons, including poverty, a lack of employment, a shortage of affordable housing, domestic violence, mental illness and drug addiction.

Homelessness has a profound effect on those who experience it. It is likely to have a negative impact on physical and mental health, sense of identity and social integration. In the case of homeless children, academic performance may be impaired as well.

Homelessness is clearly becoming an urgent problem, given the increasing numbers of people who are affected and the severity of its impact on individuals and society. In order to address the problem, its root causes need to be targeted, rather than its symptoms. Otherwise, the problem of homelessness will simply be perpetuated.

Bibliography

Task 2 Thinking about the argument

2.1 In groups of 3–4, present your additions to Andrew Student's essay. Take it in turns to explain what was weak in the essay and how each of your additions strengthens the essay.

2.2 In the same groups, discuss your work in detail.

a) Do you agree about which points need strengthening?

b) Which pieces of information are most persuasive?

c) Is the source of each piece of information shown clearly?

Task 3 Thinking about the research process

3.1 In the same group, discuss the process of researching and referencing the essay. Consider the following questions.

a) When is the best point to find sources in the essay-writing process?

b) What should you do if you cannot find appropriate sources?

c) Which part of the process did you enjoy most?

d) Which part did you find most difficult?

e) What is the most important thing you have learnt?

What advice would you give to another student who is starting this module?

Reflect

Reflect on how the essay on homelessness has been improved by the addition of your research. Then think about how the skills you have used in this research could be used in subjects such as Science, Maths, Engineering, etc.

Student notes for Unit 6

Module 10

Web work

Website 1   **Keyword searching**

http://www.sussex.ac.uk/library/infosuss/planning_a_search/index.shtml

Review
A guide to planning a search.

Task
Access the site and complete the tutorial and quiz.

Website 2   **Evaluating sources**

http://www.sussex.ac.uk/library/infosuss/evaluating_information/practical.shtml

Review
A guide to evaluating sources.

Task
Access the site and complete the tutorial and quiz.

Website 3   **Avoiding plagiarism**

http://www.princeton.edu/pr/pub/integrity/pages/plagiarism.html

Review
A good guide that shows varying grades of plagiarism from Princeton University in the USA.

Task
Access the site and complete the online activities.

Extension activities

Look at the following essay extracts and consider the differences. Which one(s) incorporate another person's ideas correctly and which would be unacceptable? Which version(s) do you prefer?

a)

> In the words of the song, "There's no place like home". Nevertheless, for a large proportion of the world's population, staying at home has become impossible. Wars, famines and religious persecution have caused many to leave their homes.

b)

> According to the old adage: "There's no place like home." (Payne 1822). However, for a large proportion of the world's population, staying at home has become unfeasible. Conflicts, famines and religious persecution, to name but a few, have caused many to desert their homes.

c)

> Payne (1822) believed that there is no place like home. This may be true for many people, but for others in economically deprived areas of the world, home has had to be abandoned.

Match these reporting verbs (a)–(e) to their effects (1)–(5)

a) claims

b) proves

c) suggests

d) illustrates

e) outlines

1. has strong evidence

2. gives examples

3. is an opinion that not everyone agrees with

4. gives the main points only

5. has weak evidence

What effect do the following reporting verbs have?

argues   asserts   believes   persuades us   points out   questions   reminds us

Glossary

Academic culture (n) The values and beliefs that exist in academic institutions, particularly those which inform and influence academic conventions.

Academic field (n) Subject area or branch of knowledge that someone may choose to study or specialise in.

Access (a site) (v) To go to a website.

APA System (n) One of a number of 'citation styles' which set out how to reference sources in a bibliography or in the body of the text.

Assignment (n) A piece of work, generally written, that is set as part of an academic course and is normally completed out of class and submitted by a set date to be assessed.

Author (n) The person who writes a book, article or other printed text, electronic article or system such as a website.

Bibliography (n) A list of references to sources cited in the text of a piece of academic writing or a book. A bibliography should consist of an alphabetical list of books, papers, journal articles and websites and is usually found at the end of the work. It may also include texts suggested by the author for further reading.

Cite (v) To acknowledge sources of ideas in your work. This may consist of an in-text reference to an author, a reference in a bibliography or footnote or a verbal reference in a talk or lecture.

Conventions (n) Widely used and accepted practices that are agreed upon. Academic conventions for research include: dividing essays and reports into sections, referencing all sources and writing a bibliography according to certain styles, such as the APA System.

Corporate author (adj) A term used to describe authorship of a text that does not have a named author (or authors), such as a report or article produced by a government department or other organisation.

Counterargument (n) An argument that opposes or makes the case against another argument.

Dissertation (n) A long essay, that may involve original research, and which is often a key component of a degree or diploma programme.

Edition (n) All the copies of a version of a published text produced at one time are known as an edition. Later editions of a text may include changes, corrections and additions so, if known, it is necessary to state the edition of a text that you cite in a bibliography.

Electronic source (n) Any text that has been accessed on the Internet or from a CD, audiocassette or video rather than from a printed source.

Essay (n) An analytical piece of academic writing that is usually quite short in length. Students are required to write essays as assignments and in exams so that their learning can be assessed.

Evaluate (v) To assess information in terms of quality, relevance, objectivity and accuracy.

Higher education (n) Tertiary education that is beyond the level of secondary education and usually offers first and higher degrees. A university is an institution of higher education.

In-text reference (n) A reference that is in the body of the text. It is normally put in brackets and is shorter than the reference in the bibliography. It should include the author's name and the year of publication as a minimum.

Journal (n) A publication that is issued at regular and stated intervals (such as every month or quarter), and which contains articles and essays by different authors. Journals include magazines and newspapers as well as academic periodicals that contain more scholarly articles on specialised topics.

Paraphrase (v) To alter a piece of text so that you restate it (concisely) in different words without changing its meaning. It is useful to paraphrase when writing a summary of someone's ideas; if the source is acknowledged, it is not plagiarism. It is also possible to paraphrase your own ideas in an essay or presentation; that is, to state them again, often in a clearer, expanded way.

Plagiarism (n) The act of presenting someone else's work, i.e., written text, data, images, recording, as your own. This includes:

- copying or paraphrasing material from any source without an acknowledgment;
- presenting other people's ideas without acknowledging them;
- working with others and then presenting the work as if it was completed independently.

Plagiarism is not always deliberate, and it is important to adopt the academic conventions of always indicating ideas and work that are not your own, and referencing all your sources correctly.

Quotation (n) A part of a text written or spoken by one author and reproduced in a text, piece of academic writing or talk by another author. When you quote someone's words or ideas, you do not change the wording at all and should put it in inverted commas ("~") to signal that it is a quotation.

Reference (n) (v) 1 (n) Acknowledgment of the sources of ideas and information that you use in written work and oral presentations. 2 (v) To acknowledge or mention the sources of information.

Research (v) (n) 1 (v) To gather information from a variety of sources and analyse and compare it. 2 (n) Information collected from a variety of sources about a specific topic.

Research question (n) A statement or question that helps you to start gathering together ideas, notes and information in a focused way in preparation for writing an essay, report, presentation or dissertation.

Search engine (n) A website comprising a large database of other websites. A search engine's spider collects Web pages and the search engine then allows visitors to do a keyword search to find useful pages.

Seminar (n) A small group discussion led by a tutor, lecturer or guest speaker. Students are expected to take an active part in the seminar.

Source (n) Something (usually a book, article or other text) that supplies you with information. In an academic context, sources used in essays and reports must be acknowledged.

Supporting argument (n) It is necessary to provide supporting evidence, arguments and statements to strengthen your ideas and opinions in an academic essay. This support may include reference to other sources, quotations and data.